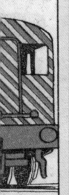

An A–Z of Laughs!

When The Dandy and Beano first appeared in
the late 1930s, they brought with them hours of
entertainment for girls and boys across Britain.
They also introduced some of the funniest and most
endearing characters in comic history.

These new characters soon became lords and ladies
of laughter, as they embarked on adventures,
embraced rebellion, and pulled numerous pranks.
This collection of strips, hand-selected from our
archive, presents some of their best moments,
showcasing the humour and hilarity that became the
heart of The Dandy and Beano!

© DCT Consumer Products (UK) Ltd 2017
D.C. Thomson and Co. Ltd,
185 Fleet Street,
London EC4A 2HS

Printed in China

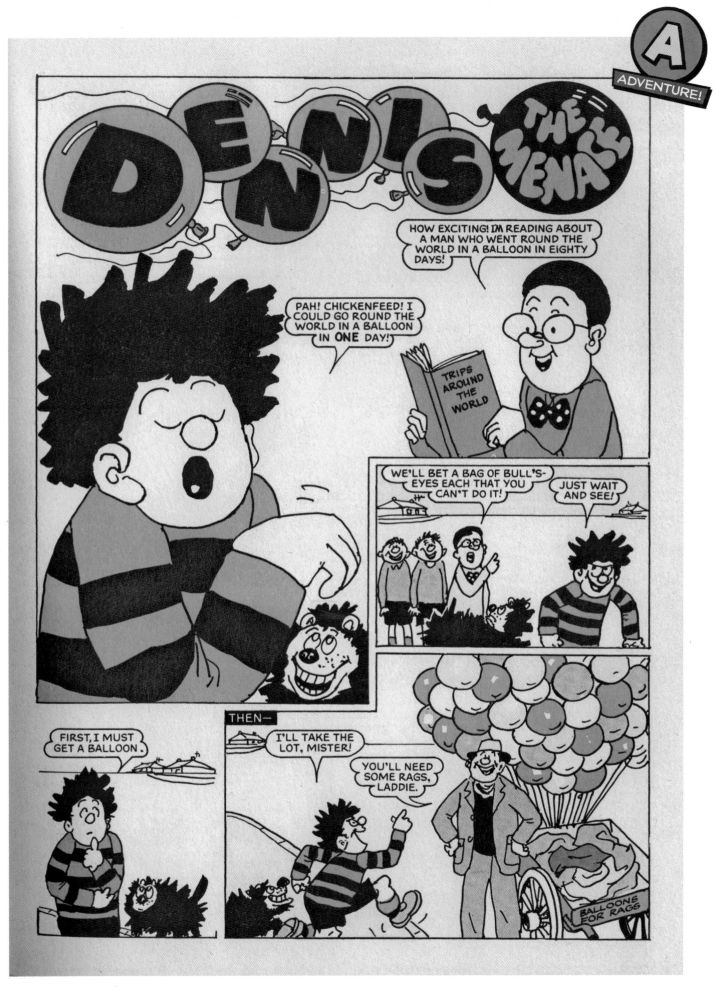

A is for Adventure!

Beano and Dandy characters often embarked on amazing adventures. In this strip from 1971, Dennis's attempt to travel around the world didn't quite go as planned...

JIMMY'S MAGIC PATCH

Jimmy, out cycling one day, spied some men competing in an Archery Competition. "This looks fun," said Jimmy to himself, and stopped to watch the unusual contest. "If they were all dressed differently and wore feathers in their hats it would just be like the days of Robin Hood and his Merry Men. Sherwood Forest must have been an exciting place." Suddenly Jimmy said out loud:—"I wish I were living in those times, and could meet Robin Hood and Maid Marion, too."

Now on Jimmy's pants there was a big patch. But it wasn't just an ordinary patch. It was a MAGIC patch. And every time Jimmy wished a wish, the patch on his pants saw that the wish was granted. It never failed to oblige Jimmy, and sure enough it worked the trick once again, and suddenly Jimmy found himself on a small path cycling through a forest. There, right in front of him, he saw two monks beating up a lad. Two horses grazed near by.

Jimmy found himself travelling through history thanks to the magic patch sewn into his shorts. In this adventure, he found himself face to face with Robin Hood!

The monks grabbed the bag that the poor lad was clutching, then mounted and rode off on the horses. Jimmy approached the dazed boy and asked if he could help. "These are robbers dressed as monks," the lad said, "and they are the same ones who are waylaying and robbing all the poor people around here. If you would like to help, ride to Robin Hood in Sherwood Forest and tell him. I will follow. My name is Edwin."

Off Jimmy went on his bicycle, speeding through the trees till he came to a small clearing. There, sure enough, were Robin Hood and some of his Merry Men, and also Maid Marion. As Jimmy drew nearer he could see they were all enjoying an afternoon of sport, but at his approach, they looked up in great surprise and wonder. Robin Hood and company, of course, had never seen such a thing as a bicycle.

At first, Robin and his followers were very wary, and then finding the excited Jimmy to be a friendly boy, they came closer. " I'll show you some trick-riding," said Jimmy, and was so thrilled at being able to show off in front of this famous man, that he quite forget the message from Edwin. Laying a narrow track of leaves round a great oak tree, Jimmy began to cycle round faster and faster. The Merry Men were awe-struck. Then Edwin entered the clearing.

Jimmy jumped from his cycle and joined the others who had clustered round Edwin. The boy was able to tell Robin Hood the direction the robbers had taken. " Would you not ride after them, Robin Hood? You are the only one who can teach them a lesson." Robin Hood looked worried. " Most of my horses are away with the rest of the Merry Men on a mission. The only two I kept for myself were stolen last night. I have no doubt those robbers took them."

"There's my bike, Robin Hood!" Jimmy cried, "I'll take you on the carrier." Robin Hood looked very doubtful at Jimmy's suggestion, but after a little persuasion finally consented. Robin was no lightweight, and it took Jimmy all his time to keep his balance. At last they were off to the cheers and laughter of the Merry Men. They sped along a woodland path. "We'll catch those rascals yet," said Jimmy, as they careered along.

Faster and faster Jimmy pedalled. On reaching the crest of a hill, Jimmy suddenly spied below the two robbers. "There they are!" he cried. "Get ready, Robin Hood!" "Look!" cried Robin, as he, too, saw them. "They are on my horses. I'll get the rascals for this, though we have to chase them for miles." Jimmy took a dim view of this remark, for already his legs were beginning to ache. But he pedalled bravely on.

The strange chase brought them to a village. Seeing his chance, Robin Hood suddenly raised himself from the carrier as high as he dared. Fitting an arrow into his bow, he took aim. Jimmy tried to steer as even a course as possible, for he knew one false move on his part would be fatal to Robin Hood's plans. Whang! The arrow shot through the air, and suddenly one of the so-called monks found himself pinned by his cloak to a huge oak tree. The horse galloped on.

Robin and Jimmy did not waste any time on the rascal pinned to the tree, for the second man, realising his danger, had put a spurt on. But just as he was passing the stocks, Robin again took aim. Whang! Another arrow flew through the air, and the second robber was unseated and pinned by his cloak to one of the posts of the stocks. The villagers, by this time, were taking an interest in the proceedings, as many of them had been victims of the robbers' cruelty.

Soon the rascals were firmly bound and led off. Robin Hood and Jimmy then picked up the robbers' sacks. The villagers gathered around, and Robin handed back the goods that had been stolen. By this time the horses, freed from the robbers, trotted back to Sherwood Forest by themselves. So Robin Hood and Jimmy had to return by bicycle— but this time Robin rode the bicycle and Jimmy was on the pillion!

And then the fun started! Robin Hood declared that this was an occasion for celebrating. And what a feast they had! There were huge roasts of beef, chickens, fruit of all kinds, and luscious tarts made by Maid Marion's fair hands. Never had Jimmy enjoyed such a picnic! He would be very loth to leave Robin Hood and his Merry Men, but he knew that sooner or later he must. At the moment, however, he was determined to enjoy himself, which he certainly did!

PANSY POTTER
IN WONDERLAND

B is for Beano!

Big Eggo was Beano's first cover star, and held the coveted position for nearly ten years!

Beano's logo and cover stars may have changed through the years,
but its humour has remained as funny as ever!

C is for Calamity!

Misfortune often plagued the Beano and Dandy cast, with no-one being unluckier than Calamity James. His first appearance, shown here, had all the elements that would make him one of Beano's funniest characters for years to come.

KORKY THE CAT

SMOKY THINKS HE'S VERY SLICK,
WHEN ON KORKY HE PLAYS A TRICK,
BUT KORKY HOOKS A TASTY DISH—
THE TRAIN WAS LOADED UP WITH FISH!

D is for Dandy!

Korky the Cat was the cover star of
The Dandy for 47 years, passing the
baton to Desperate Dan in 1984.

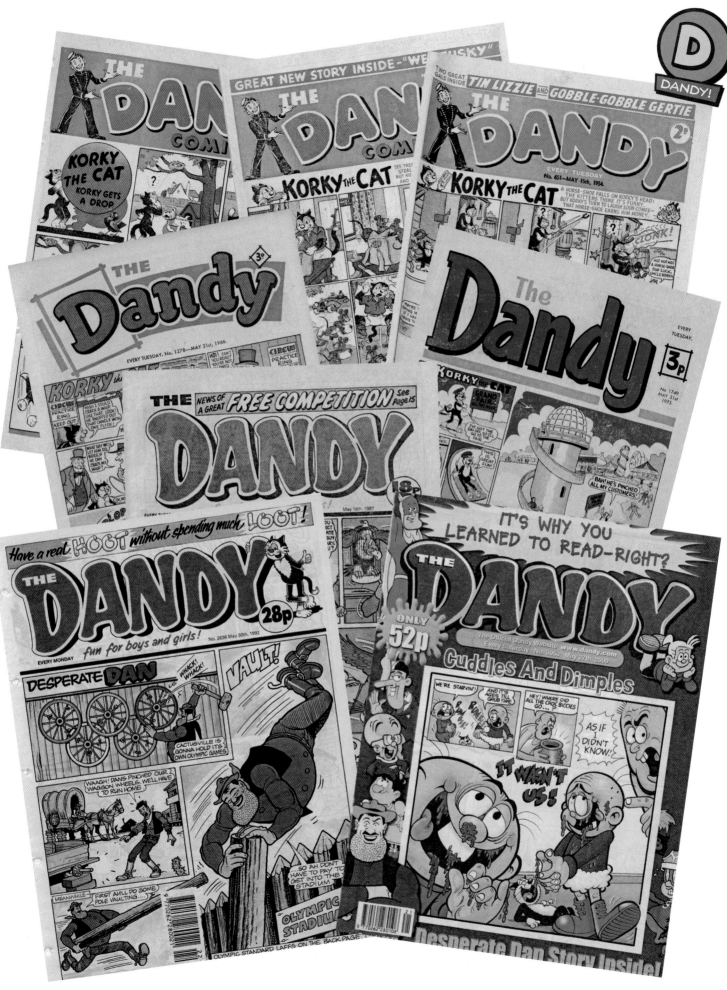

In fact, The Dandy featured only three cover stars between 1937 and 2000: Korky, Desperate Dan and the terrible toddlers, Cuddles and Dimples.

E is for Explosions!

The dynamic characters from both Beano and Dandy have a history of exploding on to the page! This early Dennis the Menace strip sees the rogue attempt his own rocket launch, which unfortunately fizzles out.

EXPLOSIONS!

THE BIG SHOW

F is for Feasts!

Food has played an important role in many of the comic strips, and The Three Bears' outrageous attempts to find feasts have given readers great laughs over the decades.

DESPERATE DAN

Dan in the street
Sees his burning feet
Holes a-making.

What can he do?
Now see him lasso.
Mast's a-shaking.

Dan has a hope!
He cuts the rope.
Ain't he daring?

Way up so high—
Right into the sky.
How's he faring?

Dan's feeling swell.
Then he gives a yell.
Why? You're asking.

With lots of din
In the ice-cream bin
Dan lies basking.

Desperate Dan is especially well known for his love of food. These two strips show the
lengths the Cactusville strongman will go to for his favourite grub!

HIC-HIC HOORAY!

G is for Gnashing!

This brilliant strip from August 1968 introduced the notorious Gnasher to Beano readers. If dogs really do look like their owners, Dennis couldn't have found a better match than this menacing mutt whose coat perfectly resembled Dennis' unruly hair.

GNASHING!
DENNIS the MENACE
GOOD IDEA, THAT. I'M A FAMOUS MENACE!
DAILY BLURP
FAMOUS AMERICAN ACTRESS FIFI FRUMP LEAVES HER FOOT AND HAND PRINTS IN CEMENT.
FIFI FRUMP
FIRST I NEED SOME CEMENT.
READY MIXED CEMENT
ADD WATER AND STIR WELL. CHORTLE!
NOW A QUICK SMOOTH OVER AND IT'S READY TO RECEIVE MY FAMOUS HAND PRINTS.
BUT—
AH! WELL DONE, DENNIS! I'VE BEEN MEANING TO GET THAT PATH CEMENTED FOR YEARS!
BUT DAD, YOU DON'T—
I'LL COVER IT UP SO NOBODY CAN LEAVE ANY MARKS ON IT.
LATER—
HOI, CURLY, GNASHER! OVER HERE A MINUTE!
NOW EVERYBODY WILL KNOW THAT DENNIS WAS HERE!
DENNIS'S DOG GNASHER
GNASHER'S MAKING HIS MARK!
HURRY UP, TORTY, OR YOU'LL GET SET IN YOUR WAYS!
THEN—
GURR! YOU'VE RUINED MY LOVELY PATH!
IT WAS MY LOVELY PATH!
GASP! MADE IT!
OOYAH!
WHUMP!
GUESS WHO'S LEFT THIS SLIPPER MARK, READERS!

Gnasher was not the only infamous dog to resemble his owner. Pup Parade introduced the Bash Street Dogs, who could be just as mischievous as their human counterparts.

POOR DOGGY!

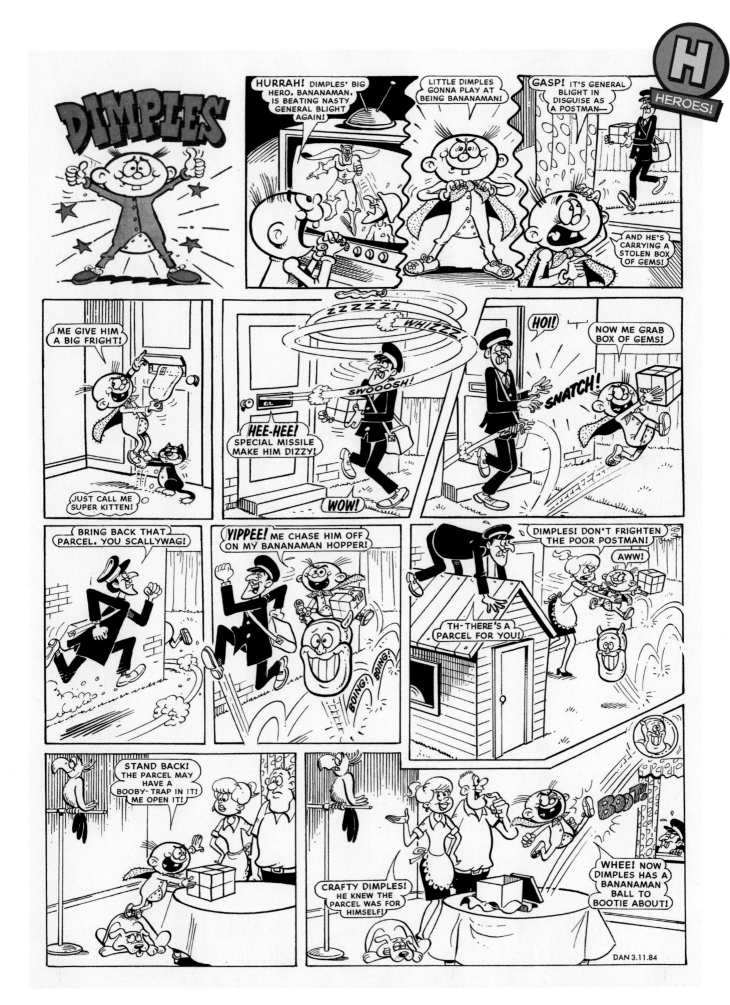

H is for Heroes!

Many heroic tales have appeared in the pages of Beano and Dandy over the decades, inspiring the younger characters. This strip shows Dimples celebrating his favourite caped character – and causing just as much calamity along the way!

MINNIE the MINX

JUMBLE SALE

YAHOO! LOOK AT THE PILE OF OLD "BEANOS" I'VE BOUGHT!

I LOVE THE SUPERHEROES THAT USED TO APPEAR IN "THE BEANO" YEARS AGO! LIKE "THE IRON FISH"...

The IronFish sailed the seven seas in search of adventure—

I'LL MAKE MY OWN IRON FISH!

ERK! WHERE'S THE DUSTBIN GONE?

AND WITH A MIGHTY LEAP, MIN'S IRON FISH...

...LANDS IN THE FISHPOND!

WAHGLUB!

I THINK I'LL BE GENERAL JUMBO INSTEAD!

JUMBO

General Jumbo had a remote-control army which he used to fight crime—

GENERAL MIN'S GOT A REMOTE-CONTROL CAR!

BNO 27.4.85

The First Adventures Of The Mysterious Superman—

THE AMAZING MR X

1—Len Manners, a private inquiry agent, sat at his desk in a tiny office by the quayside of a large English town. Len was tall and loosely built, but behind his glasses, his eyes sparkled keen and bright. Outside, the wind howled and the sea rose in giant waves. Len looked through the window at the storm.

2—Something far out at sea caught Manners' eye. Quickly he crossed to the window and took off his glasses. Instantly, Len saw away out at sea—a ship in distress. Len Manners' eyesight was so good that he could see for miles. He didn't need spectacles. Actually, they toned down his sight!

3—Leaping over to a huge book-case, Len did a strange thing. He pressed the back of a particular book. Part of the book-case swung open revealing a secret cupboard. Inside, on a hook, hung a strange costume, black skin-tights, white woollen jersey, black cloak and black mask.

4—At lightning speed Len changed from his ordinary clothes into the black skin-tight trousers, jersey and mask. A great red X was marked on the chest of the close fitting white jersey. Then Len Manners tensed his muscles and drew a deep, long breath, squaring his broad shoulders as he did so.

5—Instantly a change seemed to come over him. His muscles bulged and in place of the loose-built Manners stood a superman! For some time now Len Manners had been building up his strength and faculties. Now he was to show the world what he could do! Quickly he dived from his office window.

6—No ordinary man could have taken such a dive, but to Mr X it was nothing. He swam strongly towards the sinking ship through the mountainous seas. His strength was such that he was soon out to where the tiny trawler was slowly disappearing beneath the waves. The seamen waved to him frantically.

7—Mr X swam to the side of the stricken ship. The crew threw him a rope and the superman tied it round his body. Mr X told the seamen to attach themselves to the line and jump into the water. The crew obeyed and Mr X swam through the towering waves towards an approaching ship. A man on board the ship threw him a rope. Mr X clambered up to the rail. Hanging there, he pulled the sailors he had rescued up the side of the ship by the sheer strength of his right arm.

8—The men on the ship grabbed the shipwrecked sailors as Mr X hauled them aboard. Soon they were sitting drinking steaming mugs of hot tea. Mr X saw that the seamen were in safe hands and turned to go. An excited shout rose from the ship's crew. One or two men dashed forward to stop him. Mr X paid them no heed. He dived off the side of the ship back into the stormy sea. Mr X wanted no thanks or fuss. Also, he intended that the identity of Mr X should remain a mystery.

Considered to be Britain's first superhero, The Amazing Mr X appeared in The Dandy from 1944–1945.
His first appearance, shown here, proves everyman Len Manners' worth as a capable hero!

—What Is The Secret Of His Astounding Strength?

9—It didn't take Mr X long to reach the docks again. Feeling as fresh as ever after his terrific battle against the sea, Mr X climbed up the steps leading out of the water. The dockside was deserted except for a small boy who was playing with a ball beside some huge and heavy logs of wood. Mr X smiled.

10—Abruptly, the smile left his face. His marvellous eyesight had seen the topmost log of the pile quiver a little. Mr X realised that it was going to fall —right on top of the little boy. Mr X drew in his breath, tensed all his mighty muscles and sprang forward like a shot from a gun.

11—Down the quayside flew Mr X at an amazing speed, his arms outstretched and his eyes flashing through the holes of his black mask. His feet seemed to barely touch the ground as he sped along. No man could run as fast as he! Now he ran faster than ever he had done before!

12—Mr X reached the falling log just as it was toppling to the ground. Up flashed his hands to take the full weight of the heavy piece of wood. Muscles bulging, Mr X strove to keep the log up. It must have weighed close on a ton! The whole thing had happened so quickly that the little boy whom Mr X had saved did not know of his danger. Now his cry of fear brought some workmen running to the spot to see what was wrong. Mr X stood braced with the huge log held above him.

13—The workmen gasped in amazement when they saw Mr X holding the log up by himself. More and more men appeared on the scene. Mr X shouted for some of them to help to take the weight from him. He wanted to get away from the crowd. Half a dozen men jumped forward and took the log of wood from him. The little boy's mother had arrived and had taken care of her son. Mr X saw that he would have to do some explaining if he stayed much longer.

14—Mr X looked round to see if he could slip unseen through the crowd. It was impossible. There was no way he could escape the congratulations of the people who crowded round him. Again he breathed deeply and a surge of power ran through his body. Up into the air he leaped, right over the heads of the crowd. It was a sensational standing leap. In a moment he had flashed round a corner and was out of sight.

15—Some time later, Mr X had become just plain Len Manners. He sat at his desk in his office reading an evening newspaper. Others lay on his desk. Len grinned as he read their headlines, "WHO IS MR X?" "Well," thought Len Manners, "they'll have a lot more questions to ask before I'm finished. Mr X has just come to life. He has a lot of work to do. I'm going to make Mr X the talk of the world."

BILLY THE CAT

THE amazing story of William Grange, who is anything but the quiet, bespectacled schoolboy he appears to be. One afternoon William sees Johnny Ferguson, a fellow pupil at Burnham Academy, looking at bicycles...

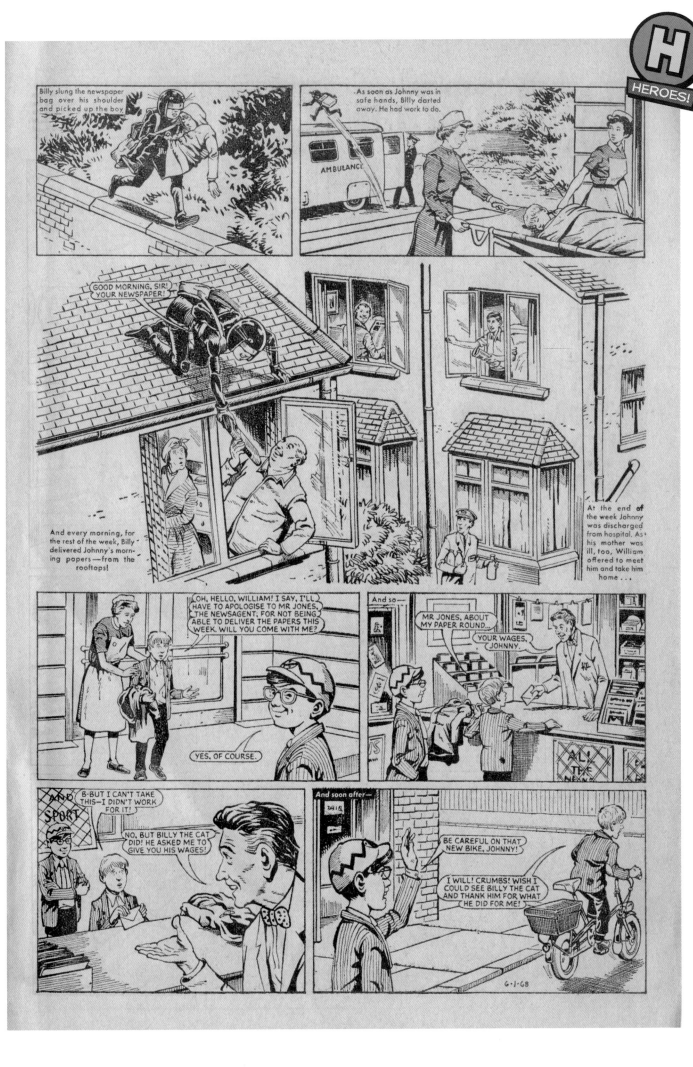

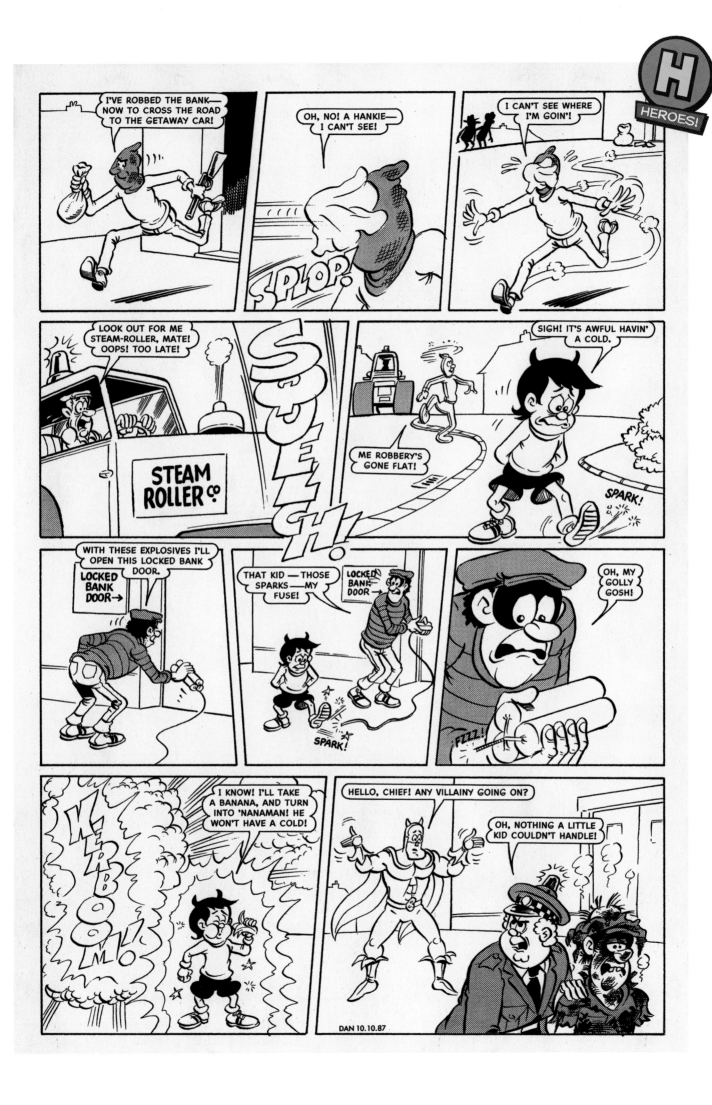

I is for Inventions!

Hilarity often ensued as the result of inventions and creative ideas in Beano and Dandy. Lord Snooty and his friends went on all kinds of adventures with Professor Screwtop!

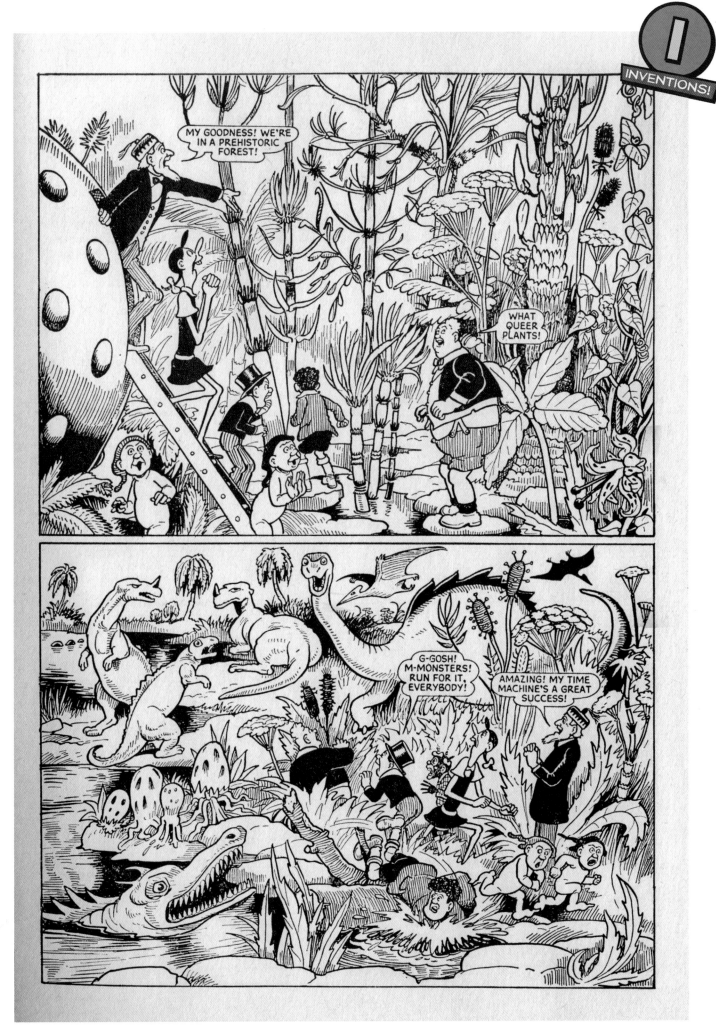

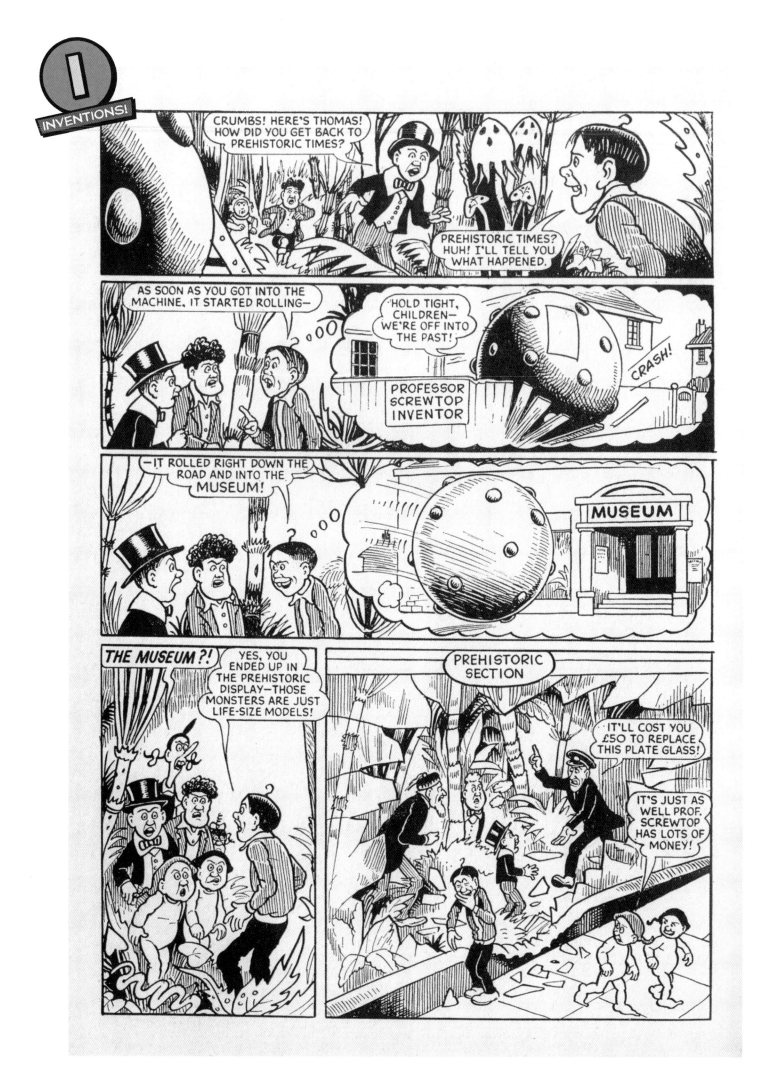

J is for Jokes!

Where would Beano and Dandy be without plenty of jokes? After the comic's stars had done their bit, the joke pages gave readers a chance to chip in with their own gags!

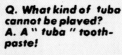

K is for Korky!

The Dandy cover star for over four decades, Korky the Cat became one of the most beloved characters in the comic. His creative thinking, prank playing, and misfortune always led to laughter, whether he was warding off bullies or trying to rid his home of pesky mice.

THE Dandy

PIE-EATERS!

Send for your BADGES! See Page 2

8p

No. 2035
November 22nd, 1980.

EVERY TUESDAY

KORKY!

KORKY!

THE BASH STREET KIDS

L is for Lessons!

School was a notorious hotspot for mischief and mayhem for many of the Beano and Dandy characters, but the most important lesson they always learned was that of laughter!

THE SMASHER

LATE FOR SCHOOL

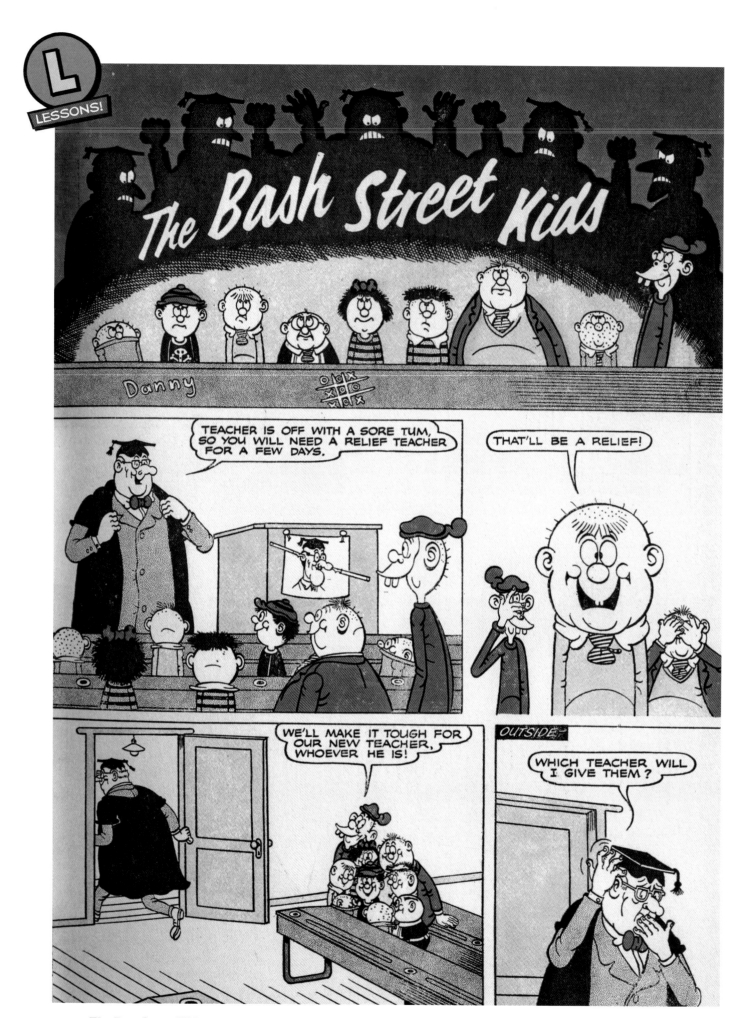

The Bast Street Kids were the most notorious classmates in all of Beanotown, often running Teacher ragged.
But in this strip, the gang learn that perhaps their teacher isn't so bad after all.

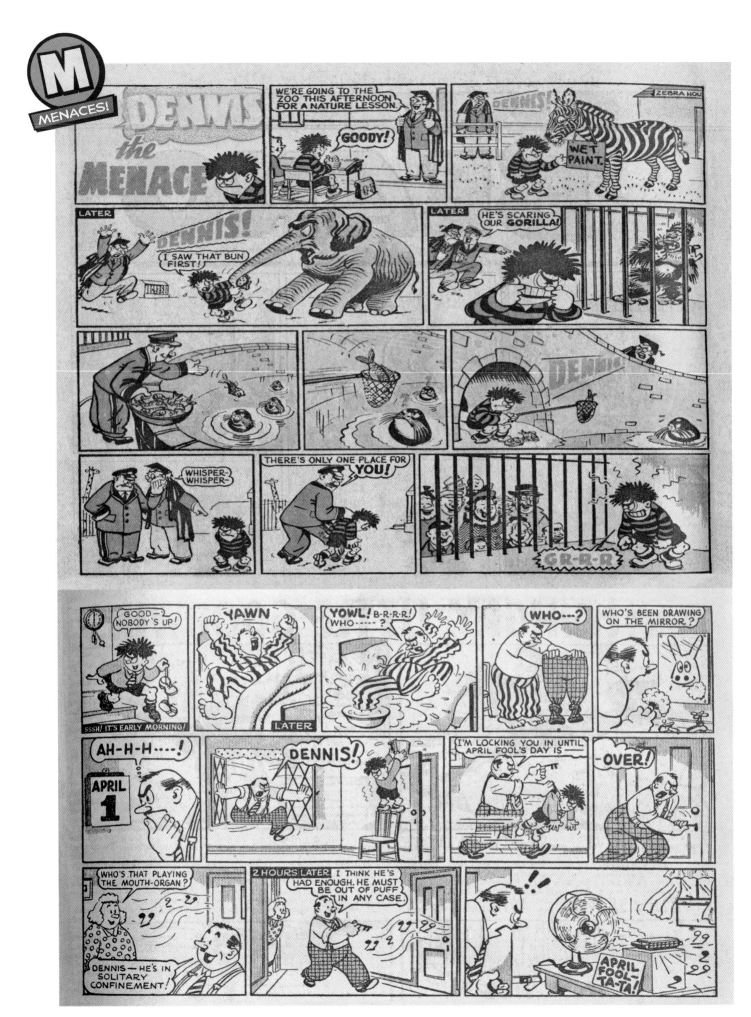

M is for Menaces!

The most notorious menace of all, Dennis, first joined Beano's crew in 1951. Now the comic's longest running strip, his striped black and red jumper and unruly hair have become a symbol for mischief across the country.

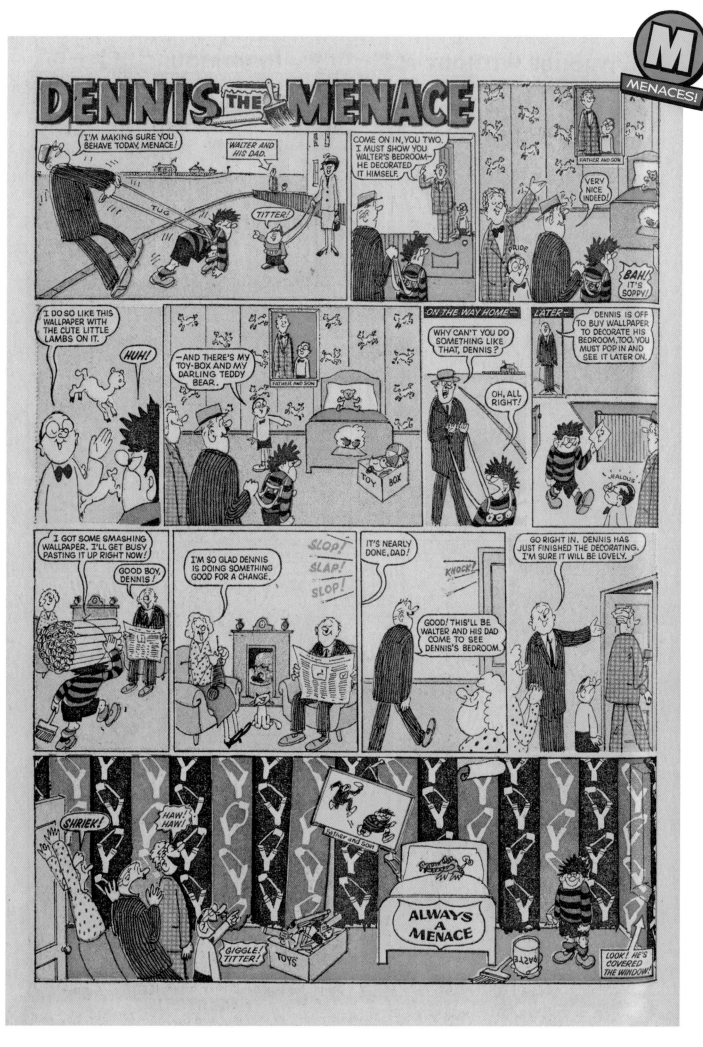

Winker WATSON

WINKER WATSON and his pals of the Third Form at Greytowers were all keen conkers players, and they knew where there was a super chestnut tree with a heavy crop of conkers. It was right in the middle of Farmer Giles' meadow, and although the farm was out of bounds, that didn't worry the boys one bit. Winker was the world's top schoolboy wangler, well used to breaking the rules laid down by the Greytowers Masters, and getting away with it!

LET'S GO AND COLLECT SOME CONKERS, LADS. THEY SHOULD BE READY BY NOW.

The boys began to shake the branches of the tree, to bring down the ripe conkers.

KEEP SHAKING, LADS.

But they brought down more than conkers! They were crowned by a shower of police truncheons!

OOPS! CAREFUL!

OW!

OO-ER!

BONK!!

The boys ran out from under the tree. And just in time too, for tumbling down after the truncheons came a bunch of bobbies! What's more, Winker recognised them.

GOSH! WE'VE SHAKEN DOWN THE SUPER AND TWO OF HIS MEN!

The Superintendent was in charge of the police college next door to Greytowers, where bobbies trained to be detectives, and he was hopping mad at Winker.

GURR! WE WERE WATCHING THE FARMHOUSE FROM UP THAT TREE BECAUSE WE HAD A TIP-OFF THAT IT'S GOING TO BE BURGLED TODAY, AND IT'S YOUR FAULT NOW IF IT HAPPENS!

Mr Creep, the boys' Form Master, was sent for, and he was even more annoyed than the Super.

THE SUPERINTENDENT HAS TOLD ME WHAT HAPPENED, AND I'LL DEAL WITH YOU BOYS WHEN WE GET BACK TO SCHOOL.

As Creepy marched the boys off, Winker stopped to pick something up.

ONE OF THE COPS FORGOT HIS TRUNCHEON. I'LL TAKE IT. IT MIGHT BE USEFUL.

As they passed another tree, Winker spotted a pair of feet and legs dangling from among the branches.

LOOK, MR CREEP, SIR! THERE'S SOMEBODY HIDING UP IN THAT TREE. I BET IT'S THAT BURGLAR THE POLICE WERE AFTER.

The Master saw his chance to earn a bit of praise from the Super, and he grabbed the weapon Winker was carrying and let fly with it.

GIVE ME THAT TRUNCHEON, WATSON, AND WE'LL SOON FIND OUT!

WHIZZ!

Creepy's aim was spot on. There was a yelp, a rustle, and a body came tumbling from the tree!

YELP! WHO THREW THAT?

BULL'S-EYE, MR CREEP, SIR! COME ON, LADS, JUMP ON HIM!

DAN. 26.10.74

But Winker and Company did not dive on Creepy's victim. In fact, they skidded to a halt when they saw who it was!

HOLD IT, LADS, IT'S ANOTHER COPPER!

Now Creepy was in trouble! It seemed the chestnut tree had not been the only one used as a spying post.

I WAS UP THAT TREE ON DUTY LIKE THE SUPERINTENDENT SAID, YOU NOSEY TEACHER, YOU!

Assaulting a police officer was a serious offence, and the Sergeant marched Creepy towards the cop college with his arm twisted up his back!

YOU'LL PROBABLY GET SIX MONTHS FOR STEALING A TRUNCHEON AND THROWING IT AT ME!

GOODBYE, MR CREEP, SIR.

The lads were free to return to the chestnut tree now and pick up all those conkers. Some beauties there were! The Third Formers got busy shelling them and threading them on strings.

After a while, the limping Super and his injured men returned. And as they did so, Winker caught sight of the very thing they'd been waiting for.

LOOK, SIR, THERE'S A MAN CLIMBING OUT OF THE FARMHOUSE WINDOW!

The bobbies gave chase. But with all their aches and pains and bandaged limbs, they could do no better than limp in pursuit.

AFTER HIM, MEN, AS QUICK AS WE CAN!

Winker laughed as he watched the limp-along lawmen. Then a plan to help came into his head and he turned to his pals.

QUICK, LADS, GIVE ME YOUR STRINGS OF CONKERS!

Winker tied two or three knots and the strings of conkers became something like a South American bolas. The wangler twirled it round his head, took careful aim, then let go.

WHIZZ-Z!

Bull's-eye! Or rather burglar's-feet! Winker's weapon twirled around the man's ankles, making him nose-dive to the ground.

WHIZZ-Z!

OOPS!

By the time the limping bobbies arrived, the burglar was flattened under the weight of three of his schoolboy captors.

WELL DONE, LADS! THAT'S THE VILLAIN WE WERE AFTER!

The Super was delighted at catching the robber. And for once he praised Winker Watson for the part the wangler had played. He seemed to have forgotten that the bobbies would have captured their man themselves if Winker had not interfered in the first place!

...AND AS A REWARD, YOU BOYS CAN HAVE ALL THE CONKERS YOU WANT, AND WHAT'S MORE, I THINK I'LL KEEP MR CREEP LOCKED UP ALL DAY!

OH, SIR, HOW GOOD OF YOU! AND I THINK HE DESERVES IT TOO!

DAN 26.10.74

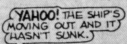

JONAH

This will turn out to be a short trip — my boats always sink.

Yahoo! The ship's moving out and it hasn't sunk.

Did you cast-off from the shore?

Er...no—but we're not sinking are we?

No—but the jetty is, you twit!

CRA-ACK!

ROGER THE DODGER

Why so glum, mum?

Those dreadful bores, the Braggs, are coming for the evening, Roger. I'd give a pound to get rid of them.

£1

I've a dodge!

WHEN THE GUESTS ARRIVE— Hello, Mr and Mrs Bragg! I'm just going to practise my violin. I hope I don't disturb you.

Of course not, Roger. You go ahead.

AND SO—IN THE LIVING ROOM— Me-yow! Ee-ow-wi' screech!

Heh-heh! These cats I've collected should do the trick!

BUT IN THE PARLOUR— Screech!! I hope you didn't mind our asking for the cotton-wool ear-plugs, old boy! Now as I was saying— blah! blah!

Yowl! Squeal!

I can't stand it!

FIVE MINUTES LATER—

Blah-blah!

Fed up

I'll switch on the T.V.

Still there, eh? This calls for Dodge Nº 717.

AT THE FRONT GATE— The bull's-eyes are on me, Tom. But I want you to nip up on our roof and give the TV aerial a good shaking!

O.K., Roger! It's a deal!

BUT DODGE Nº 717 FAILS TOO! Shocking reception, old boy. We never get that sort of thing on our set.

Tut, tut!

I'm going into the kitchen to see about dinner, dad. Perhaps you can entertain me Bragg by letting him tell you about his marvellous new lawn-mower.

By Jove, yes! I almost forgot about that!

Gloom

Roger! What's the idea of boiling up all that glue and old rubber?

Dodge Nº 54, mum! They'll think the smell is their dinner cooking—and go home.

Glue

Phew!—What a pong! If that's our dinner I'll have to think fast!

Er— look here, old boy! How about having dinner out? I know the very place.

Umph!

AND SO AT THE HOTEL DE POSH— Order what you like, folks! This is on me! Money's no object!

Whisper—Roger! Get rid of them! I don't care how you do it, but get rid of them!

Leave it to me, dad. There's a super dodge coming up any minute now!

HOTEL POSH

ROGER DODGES UNDER THE TABLE

This should do the trick!

AND THIS TIME— SHRIEK!

MICE!

?

It's working!

You brought these mice along on purpose. Out you go!

They've gone, and I've earned that pound!

Take it, Roger! It's my last one, but it's worth it to get rid of old Bragg! Ha! Ha! Ha!

BUT WHEN ROGER GOES— B-Bill? But old Bragg was going to pay! I-I haven't any m-money with me!

Your bill, sir!

Is that so?

No slacking, there! You have to wash enough dishes to cover the cost of a four-course dinner for five.

One of Roger's dodges would get me out of this — if only I could remember one!

Little Plum

ME HEAP HUNGRY.

STUFFED BEAR FOR DELIVERY TO MUSEUM

CRUMP

HANK'S DELIVERY SERVICE

COO! UM STUFFED BEAR!

STUFFED BEAR FOR DELIVERY TO MUSEUM

CHIEFY

KEEP OUT

CHIEFY'S HAVING UM BATH!

A-A-A-AGH!

HEH! HEH!

ME HIDE UNDER UM BATH TILL UM SAVAGE BEAR VAMOOSES!

LATER

PLUM! I WANT YOU TO TRACK DOWN UM SAVAGE BEAR!

LITTLE PLUM

A-A-AGH! HERE IT IS AGAIN—OWCH!

LITTLE PLUM

REWARD OF UM SMALL TUCK HAMPER FOR CAPTURE OF SAVAGE BEAR DEAD OR ALIVE

HUH! UM SMALL TUCK HAMPER'S NO GOOD! I'M HEAP HUNGRY!

CRUNCH

REWARD SMALL HAMPER CAPTURE SAVAGE DEAD O

THAT'S BETTER!

REWARD OF UM BIG TUCK HAMPER FOR CAPTURE OF SAVAGE BEAR DEAD OR ALIVE

I'LL STICK UM ARROWS IN UM STUFFED BEAR THEN CALL CHIEFY!

YOU GETTUM REWARD, BRAVE PLUM!

TUCK

M is for Minxes!

Girls proved they could certainly keep up with the boys in Beano and Dandy! Little Angel Face used her sweet persona as a clever cover whenever she needed to outsmart the bullies.

Minnie the Minx first appeared in 1953, ready to prank anyone who got in her way. Her smart plans and mischievous attitude placed her firmly at the heart of Beano, often out-menacing her co-stars.

PIRATE QUEEN

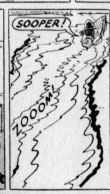

KEYHOLE KATE

"Oh, there's a golfer," Katy cried,
As she a man in plus-fours spied.
To hole a ball he tried and tried.

The golfer then began to bawl,
"This bally hole is far too small,
I can't putt in my ball at all."

"Now just a moment, mister, please,"
Our Kate replied, with perfect ease.
"I think I know a useful wheeze."

She went off with a plan all made,
And when returning brought a spade.
"The hole I'll now enlarge," she said.

And now of course as you can see,
Our Kate began to dig with glee.
The golfer cried, "Oh, dearie me!"

"It will be easy now," Kate said.
"I've made a large keyhole instead."
The golfer, not the ball, lay dead.

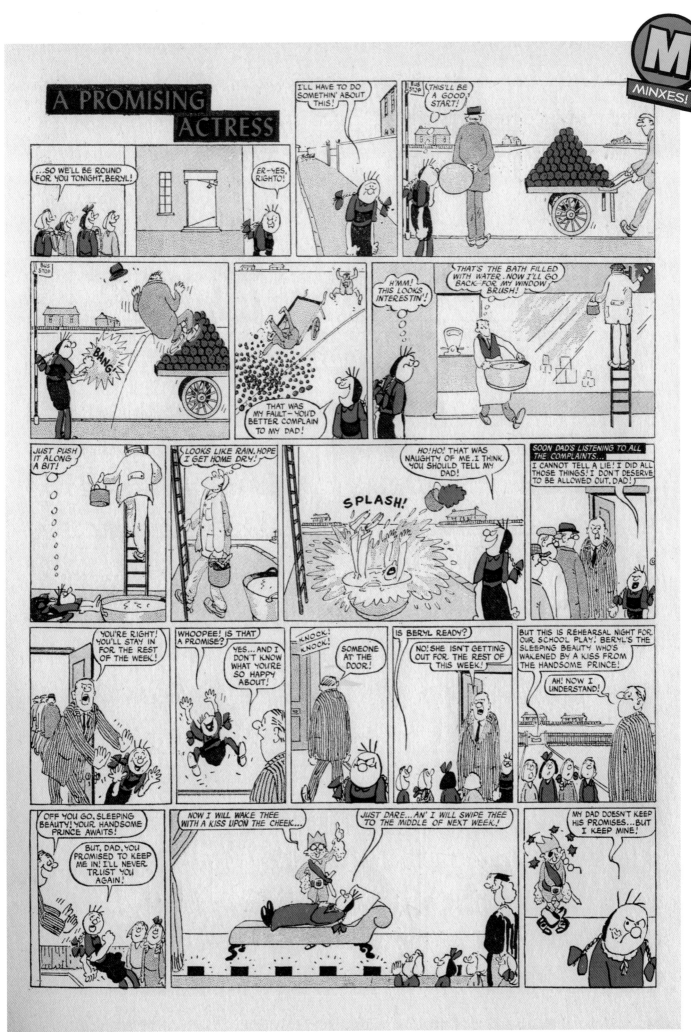

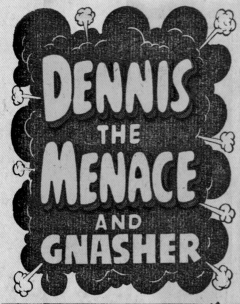

N is for Noise!

Loud characters and noisy nonsense has caused plenty of laughter over the decades.

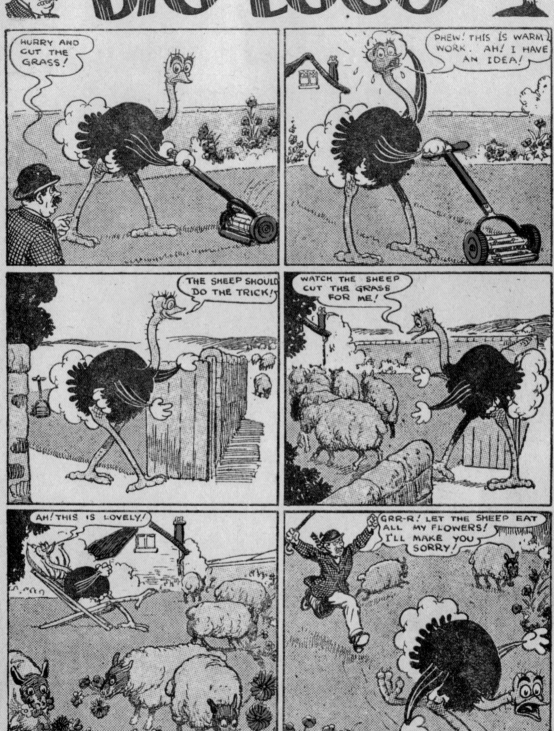

Big Eggo might be rather "green," but he had no intention of mowing the lawn all the same. And he couldn't help feeling a bit "sheepish" when he woke up and was chased by his angry boss.

O is for Outdoors!

Plenty of fun was to be had outdoors in these classic strips. With so much of the world to explore, the laughs were limitless.

BODGER the BOOKWORM

I KNOW—I'LL CLIMB UP THIS TREE AND READ THE TITLE WITH DAD'S FIELD GLASSES

THAT LOOKS LIKE AN INTERESTING BOOK THAT HORACE NEXT DOOR IS READING. WONDER WHAT IT'S CALLED?

LET'S SEE! I CAN JUST ABOUT MAKE IT OUT.

CRACK!

AARGH! THE BRANCH COULDN'T STAND MY WEIGHT!

I'LL GET A BETTER VIEW FROM THE TOP OF THE GREENHOUSE.

EEK! THE GLASS IS SLIPPIER THAN I THOUGHT!

GLUG!

HORACE! PUT DOWN THAT BOOK AND COME IN FOR YOUR LUNCH!

RIGHT, MUM!

GOOD! NOW'S MY CHANCE TO NIP OVER THE FENCE AND LOOK AT THE TITLE.

BAH!

CLIMBING FOR BEGINNERS

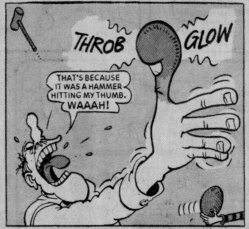

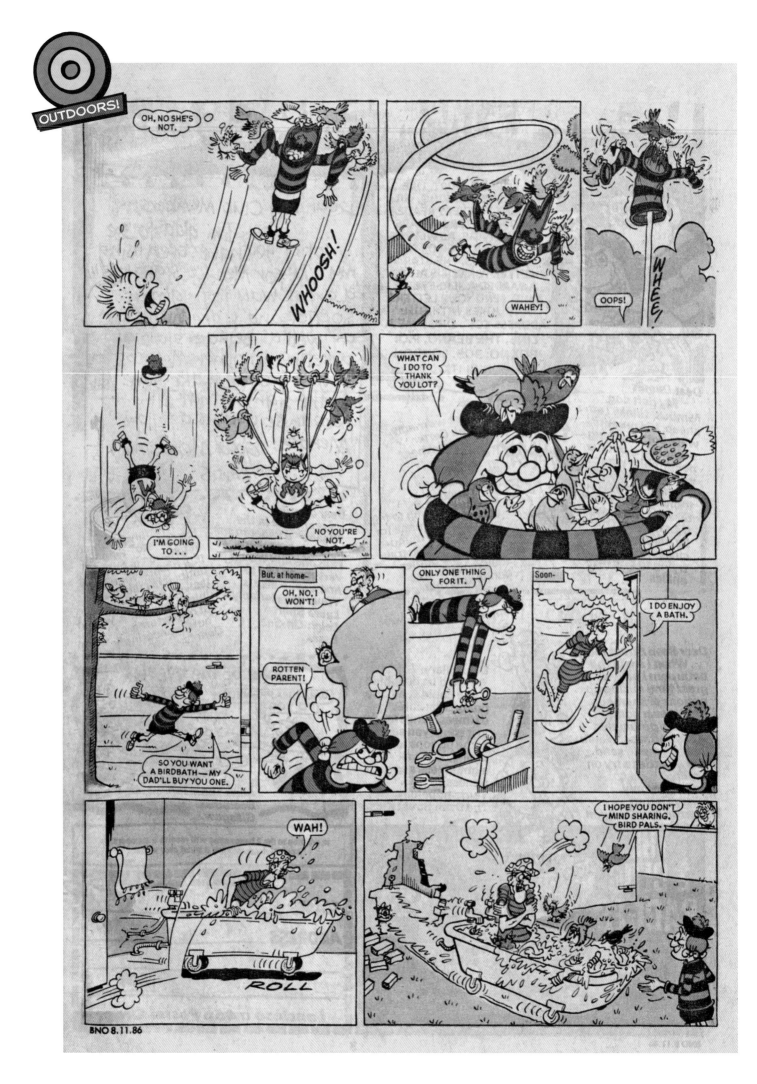

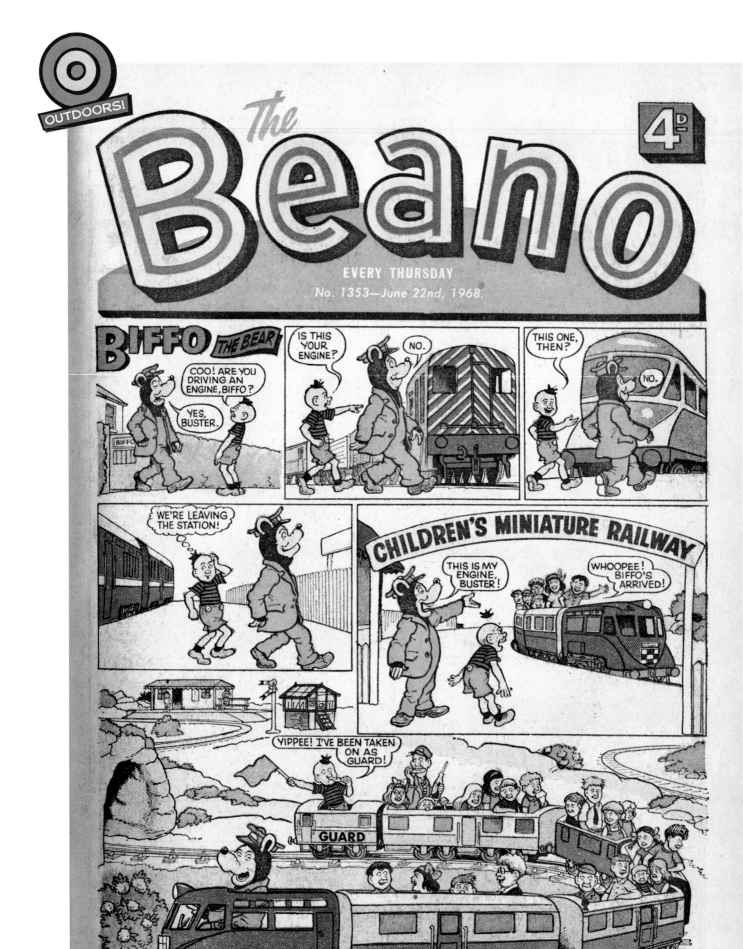

PODGE

" Now walk up kids. Your weight I'll guess
   Or give your money back.
I'm seldom wrong, I will confess
   I've got the proper knack."

So Podge stepped up, " You can't guess mine
   If I wear Dad's top hat."
" Of course I could, that's in my line.
   There ain't much weight in that."

" I'll just run home," said Podge in glee,
   " And get the old man's topper."
The man said, " O.K. that suits me,
   And don't forget your copper."

Young Podge comes back with top hat, new.
   " Now tell my weight, sir, please."
" I think you will be five stone two,"
   The smart man said with ease.

Podge stepped on to the scales to see,
   The hand whizzed round too far.
" You're seven stone two. Oh goodness me,"
   The man cried, " Here's your bar."

Now Podge is pleased as pleased can be.
   He walks off hat in hand,
And on his head a weight you see.
   His trick was really grand.

P is for Pranks!

Pranks have played a central role in Beano and Dandy since the comics first appeared in the late 1930s, almost every character having an arsenal of street-smart practical jokes they can deploy to win the day!

Great News About "THE IRON FISH" Inside

THE BEANO

2D

EVERY THURSDAY.   No. 466. JUNE 23rd, 1951.

GREEDY PIGG

BLACK BOB ON ROARING REEF

BLACK BOB and his master, Andrew Glenn, were spending a holiday in a little fishing village on the east coast. Lodging in the same cottage was Professor John Rusack, a naturalist who was studying wild life along the shore. One morning Glenn went to visit a friend while Bob and the Professor did some exploring on the rocks.

2—When Rusack came to a line of rocks known as Roaring Reef he knelt down and groped about on the bottom of a pool. Then he pulled out his arm. In his hand he had a shell, but it wasn't a winkle that was in it. Living in the shell was a hermit crab. It was the first time Black Bob had seen such a thing, and he wrinkled his nose and backed away from the crab's sharp pincers. The Professor laughed as he put it back in the pool.

3—"That's just a little hermit crab," he said. "But it will grow bigger. When it does it will have to leave this shell and move into a bigger one." While the Professor was talking he was walking on across Roaring Reef. Perhaps he was a bit careless, not watching where he was putting his feet. Anyway he trod on a slippery patch of seaweed. His feet shot from under him and he fell sideways, flinging out his arms.

4—It was so sudden that he could not save himself, and the side of his head hit a rock with a fearful crack. White-faced, he struggled to his knees, but the effort was too much for him. With a groan he fell forward on his face. Black Bob whined anxiously, but the Professor didn't move. He had been stunned, and lay there unconscious, heedless of Bob's alarmed barking, and the menacing roar of the waves beating on the reef.

Q is for Quests!

As well as funny stories, Beano and Dandy featured the bravest characters who often embarked on dangerous quests. One of the most valiant adventurers was Black Bob.

5—Anxiously Black Bob licked Rusack's face, but not even an eyelid flickered. The faithful collie kept trying to revive his friend, and for half an hour he pawed and barked at the senseless Professor. Then Black Bob sensed danger. He looked about him and whined in dismay. In that half-hour the tide had come in and surrounded them. It was still rising fast. Very soon the rock they were on would be completely under water.

6—Black Bob waited no longer. He dived into the sea and swam off to fetch help. There was no path up the cliffs here, and Bob was forced to swim right along the base of them until he was opposite the village, where a stone jetty jutted out into the sea. Bob made for it and clambered up the steps. Sitting on the jetty were two fishermen repairing their nets. Maybe they would be able to help him save the Professor.

7—Bob ran up to the fishermen, barking excitedly. He pulled at one man's jersey with his teeth, and the fisherman turned with a shout and struck out at him. "Hey, let go!" Black Bob backed away, but he kept looking at the fisherman and barking. "What's wrong with that dog, Tom?" said the other man. "It's dripping wet. Looks as if it's been in the sea. I wonder what it wants? It's excited about something."

8—Black Bob looked up and down the jetty, wondering what to do next. There were empty fish boxes and lobster pots scattered all over the place. Then Bob caught sight of a barrow. He ran to it and started to push it towards the edge of the jetty. One of the fishermen jumped to his feet, and rushed forward to stop the collie. But the man was too late. Bob pushed the barrow over the edge, then jumped into the sea after it.

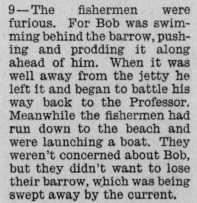

9—The fishermen were furious. For Bob was swimming behind the barrow, pushing and prodding it along ahead of him. When it was well away from the jetty he left it and began to battle his way back to the Professor. Meanwhile the fishermen had run down to the beach and were launching a boat. They weren't concerned about Bob, but they didn't want to lose their barrow, which was being swept away by the current.

10—The men had to row quite a distance to catch up with the barrow, and when they reached it one of them glanced around. " I wonder what happened to the dog?" he muttered. Then he saw the collie's black-and-white head bobbing up and down on the waves—and just beyond Bob his keen fisherman's eyes spotted a light coloured object on a rock. It was Rusack. Just then Bob reached the rock and clambered on to it.

11—" Dave," said Tom, the elder of the men, excitedly clutching his companion, "there's somebody on Roaring Reef. That's why the dog pushed the barrow into the sea. He wanted to bring us here." They left the barrow and rowed as swiftly as they could to the rock. And they were just in time. As they lifted Professor Rusack into the boat a wave broke over the rock, and minutes later it was out of sight.

12—The fishermen took the Professor back to his cottage, and when Glenn returned he was told how Bob had rescued Rusack. While they were talking, a crab scuttled into the cottage. It was part of the morning's catch and had escaped from an out-house. But Bob didn't like the look of the crab's pincers. He backed away. As he did so the Professor laughed. Bob was glad, for it meant that his friend was all right again.

THE IRON FISH

DANNY and Penny Gray are living in Sunport with their Uncle Jim, while their father, a scientist, is on an Arctic expedition. The youngsters are the proud owners of a marvellous Iron Fish, which can swim, leap and dive better than a real swordfish.

It was a fine afternoon and many anglers were out on Sunport River. But none knew that a very strange fish indeed lurked in the dark water.

GOSH! WE'VE GIVEN THAT CHAP A FRIGHT—AND ALL THE FISH, TOO, I RECKON!

Farther upriver, the Iron Fish drew into the bank beside the cottage of an old friend of the youngsters, Dan McCabe, the local water bailiff.

HELLO, KIDS!

HELLO, MR McCABE! WE'VE COME UPRIVER TO WATCH THE SALMON. WE MIGHT LEARN A FEW SWIMMING TRICKS FROM THEM!

GOOD IDEA! BUT I'M WATCHING FOR SOMETHING ELSE— SALMON POACHERS!

Some time later, in a large pool—

THERE ARE CERTAINLY SOME WHOPPERS DOWN HERE, PENNY!

Suddenly—

GOSH! HAND-GRENADES!

The two youngsters were stunned by the explosions and the Iron Fish sank to the river bed. But many dead salmon floated to the surface.

LOOKS LIKE ANOTHER GOOD HAUL, BOYS!

When Danny regained consciousness, he immediately brought the Fish to the surface to investigate.

LET'S GET OUT OF HERE!

LOOK, PENNY! SALMON POACHERS!

THEY'RE GETTING AWAY, PENNY! HEADING FOR THE LAKE ABOVE THE LOCK-GATES BY THE LOOKS OF IT!

WE CAN'T FOLLOW THEM NOW, CAN WE?

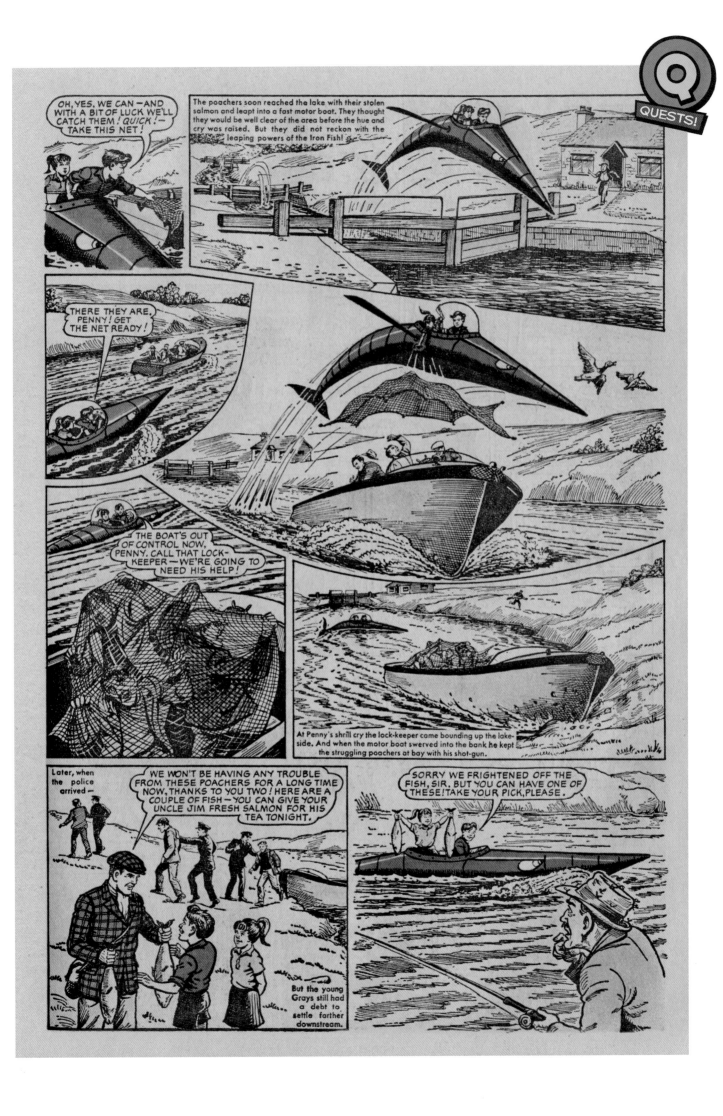

BRASSNECK

CHUCKLER Charley Brand and his wonderful metal pal, Brassneck, were helping Hotrod Harris to repair his champion car for the big Stock Car race that afternoon.

DO YOU NEED ANY TOOLS OUT OF HERE, MR HARRIS?

YES! BRING THE BOX OVER, BRASSNECK!

But a gang of twisters were jealous of Hotrod's prowess. They planned to stop him taking part. Suddenly an armour-clad car came charging like a tank towards the chums.

HEY! THAT CAR LOOKS OUT OF CONTROL!

Brassneck's electric brain box switched to full power. Acting like lightning, the metal lad grabbed two planks and placed them against Hotrod's car to make a ramp.

I HOPE THIS WORKS!

WHEE! The fast-moving car shot up the ramp, clean over the roof of Hotrod's vehicle.

WOW! WHAT'S HAPPENING?

GOSH! WE COULD HAVE BEEN KILLED!

The flying car plunged into a duckpond!

AARGH!

The two rogues, Speedy Carter and Talespin Wheeler, scrambled from the foul-smelling pond.

HO-HO! SERVES THEM RIGHT!

WHAT A PONG! THERE MUST BE A BOX OF OLD STINK BOMBS LYING IN THAT POOL!

After drying themselves out, Speedy had another idea.

I'VE GOT IT! WE'LL DRESS UP AS COPS!

In bobbies' uniforms, Speedy and Talespin tackled Hotrod. But Brassneck was suspicious of the "cops".

HAVE YOU GOT A LICENCE FOR YOUR CAR?

ER—NO!

HMM! THAT'S FUNNY! COPS DON'T USUALLY WEAR FOOTBALL SOCKS AND WINKLE-PICKERS!

The "bobbies" ordered the vehicle to be towed away.

I'M AFRAID WE'LL HAVE TO TOW YOUR CAR OFF! PUT THAT HOOK ROUND THE BUMPER, BOY!

Brassneck pretended to fix the hook round the bumper of Hotrod's car.

GOOD! NOW WHILE HE'S NOT LOOKING..........

But as soon as the "bobbies" turned their backs, the metal lad wound the hook round a tree!

THAT'LL FIX 'EM!

HO-HO! WELL DONE, BRASSNECK! THAT'LL TEACH THEM A LESSON!

YEEOW!

When the tow-lorry moved off, with Talespin at the wheel, CRE-E-EAK! CRR-A-A-SH! The tree crashed down on top of the lorry!

As the rogues staggered off, Brassneck removed the tree from the roadway.

I'LL SOON LIFT THIS LOT OUT OF THE WAY!

R is for Rebels!

Rebellion was championed in the pages of Beano and Dandy comics! These chaotic characters rarely followed rules. Jolly Roger often fell foul of Captain Crossbones by plotting his own course – rather than the Captain's orders!

Dennis the Menace is the archetypal rebel, and this strip shows him making the headlines at Beanotown's TV Studios. He runs riot until encountering the only thing he's truly scared of... Dad's slipper!

S is for Sports!

Sports have always been central to Beano and Dandy. Ball Boy always had fun on the football pitch – even when the odds were against him.

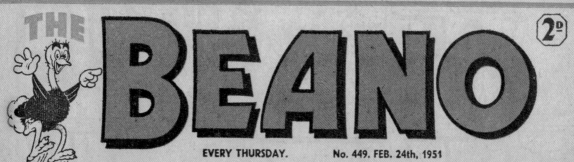

KORKY THE CAT

T is for Terrible!

Ivy first appeared in 1985. Spurred on by her hero, Dennis, this terrible toddler caused trouble for all of Beanotown and quickly became a readers' favourite.

IVY the TERRIBLE

I'LL SHOW ALL OF YOU TERRORS OUT THERE SOME GREAT PLACES TO HAVE TANTRUMS!

CAN I HAVE SWEETS, MUM?

NO — THESE ARE FOR YOUR DAD'S BIRTHDAY!

I WANT SWEETS — WAAH!

WAH!

STOMP

THUD

HERE — HAVE THIS!

PLOP!

A SWEET SHOP'S A GREAT PLACE FOR A TANTRUM!

SLURP!

SUCK

I'M LOCKING YOU IN YOUR ROOM FOR BAD BEHAVIOUR!

THUD!

WHAAAA!

BOOT!

GRAAAAAGH!

THUD!

CRASH!

G—GASP!

PLOP!

OUT — WHILE THE HOUSE IS STILL STANDING!

FREE — IT WORKED!

Soon—

I WANT SOME FLOWERS!

YUGH! TIME FOR A TANTRUM!

I HATE SOPPY SHOPS!

SIGH! A FLOWER SHOP'S A BAD PLACE TO THROW A TANTRUM!

8NO 11.10.86

Ivy wasn't the only terrible youth in Beanotown.
The Bash Street Kids were a terror for any teacher!

U is for Underdogs!

Underdogs were always the heroes of Beano and The Dandy with a full cast of characters who rose to the challenge – no matter what it was!

BULLY BEEF AND CHIPS

UNDERDOGS!

BULLY BEEF and CHIPS

V is for Victory!

Whether the wins were big or small, these characters' exploits often ended in victory!

VICTORY!

Korky follows the trail—

'GAMEKEEPERS' TRAINING SCHOOL'

HEY! WHAT'S THIS?

JUMP TO IT!

SO **THAT'S** WHERE ALL MY LOGS WENT—TO BUILD A TRAINING CIRCUIT FOR NEW GAMEKEEPERS!

Just then—

HERE ARE THE MEN'S SNACKS!

LAY THEM DOWN THERE, JUST NOW!

I WONDER WHAT'S IN HERE?

THEY TOOK MY LOGS SO NOW I'M HELPING MYSELF TO THEIR **CHOCOLATE LOGS!**

DESPERATE DAN

W is for Whizz Kids!

The fastest kid in the comics, Billy Whizz ran rings around everyone from his first appearance in 1964.

X is for eXtraordinary!

Beano and Dandy undoubtedly featured some of the most extraordinary characters in British comics, capable of unbelievable feats.

A Thief Captured By The Mysterious, Breath-Taking Superman—
THE AMAZING MR X

1—"B-r-r-r b-r-r-r" when the phone in Len Manners' office. Len, a private inquiry agent, picked up the instrument. "Sir Roger Harkness calling," came the voice from the telephone. "One of my most valuable pictures has been stolen from my house in the country. Can you come down right away?"

2—Half-an-hour later, Len was landing his private 'plane on an aerodrome near Sir Roger's house. As he climbed out of the cockpit of his 'plane, Len Manners took off his spectacles. He really didn't need them. This loosely-built young man had amazing eyesight. He could see for miles, quite clearly.

3—Now Len Manners saw something which attracted his attention. Right over at the other side of the 'drome a man was busy working on his 'plane. He was wearing a pair of shoes with a very peculiar pattern on the soles. "H-m-m, I've never seen shoes like these before," thought Len.

4—A taxi took Len Manners right out to the country house of Sir Roger Harkness. Sir Roger showed the detective the frame from which the picture had been stolen and told him all he knew about the theft. "There's very little to go on," said Len, "but give me a clear field and I'll see what I can do."

5—Len Manners left the rich man and went into the garden. Here he took a bundle of queer clothes from his case. When he had donned the black skin-tight trousers, white jersey, flowing black robe and a mask, Len Manners was no longer Len Manners. He had become Mr X, the superman!

6—Faint marks on the stone paving caught Mr X's eye. No ordinary man could have seen them. Mr X's amazing eyesight had come to his aid already! He peered close. The marks were footprints—footprints of shoes with a queer pattern exactly the same as those of the man at the aerodrome!

7—Mr X straightened up. Could the man with the queer shoes be the thief? Mr X decided to take a long chance on it. Flexing his muscles, Mr X breathed deeply. Some hidden power surged through his body. His muscles bulged and his eyes flashed. The superman was off his mark like lightning. He had to get to the aerodrome before the crook flew off in his 'plane. He flashed over the fields at a terrific speed. Mr X was determined that the crook should not escape with the picture.

8—Mr X was easily the finest runner alive. Now he went all out. A wide river loomed up in front of him, barring his path. Mr X jumped before he even reached the bank, hurtling himself through the air. The superman landed safely on the other side and sped on. He had cleared a jump of over thirty feet without turning a hair! A man fishing on the river bank, fell off his seat in sheer surprise. One moment Mr X was flashing overhead, the next he was gone.

9—At last the aerodrome came in sight. It was surrounded by a very high fence. The superman refused to waste time by going round to the gate. Never faltering in his stride, he leaped upwards. His legs tucked up beneath him, the superman cleared the twelve foot fence with inches to spare. Startled cries came from aerodrome officials who saw the weird figure's amazing jump. They watch dumbfounded as Mr X landed on his feet and sped towards a 'plane preparing to take off.

10—Mr X had spotted the crook in his 'plane. He was revving up the engine before taking off. Mr X had arrived just in time! As it was, it would take the superman all his time to stop the crook from getting his 'plane into the air. Mr X streaked towards the 'plane. His arms were outstretched ready to grasp the tail of the aeroplane and prevent it from taking off. Mr X knew he would need all his strength to prevent the crook escaping once the 'plane started to move down the runway.

11—The crook's aeroplane started to move just as Mr X reached it. The superman managed to grip the tail of the machine. Planting his feet firmly on the ground, Mr X braced himself against the pull of the powerful engine. The engine roared, trying to pull the man, who was holding it back, into the air. The crook pilot didn't know what was wrong—until he looked back. When the thief saw Mr X he was dumbfounded.

12—In his panic, the crook opened the throttle as wide as he could. The engine roared like a mad thing. Mr X nearly had his arms torn out of their sockets. Something had to go—Mr X or the 'plane. It was the 'plane! There came the sound of rending wood and metal and the tail of the 'plane came away in Mr X's hands. The rest of the 'plane plunged forward, dived into the ground and toppled over with a crash.

13—Mr X had fallen backwards to the ground but he quickly picked himself up. The crook's 'plane was lying upside down. Mr X raised it aloft with one hand and dragged the crook and his bag out of the cockpit. With the crook under his arm Mr X raced off before the aerodrome officials could stop him.

14—Back at Sir Roger's house, Mr X locked the crook in a cellar while he changed back into the clothes of Len Manners. The stolen picture was in the man's bag all right. Now, Len wished to keep his identity as Mr X a secret. He did not wish the police to interfere. Len went to Sir Roger.

15—"You can have your picture back immediately," Len said. "But I'd like you to go no further with the case." Sir Roger agreed and Len brought out the stolen painting and the thief. Len set the letter free—he had lost his 'plane, so he was punished enough. And Mr X still remained a mystery!

Y is for Yuletide!

Christmas granted the perfect opportunity for the girls and boys of the comics to decide whether they would be naughty or nice. Mischief usually triumphed!